VERRAZANO

EXPLORER
OF THE ATLANTIC COAST

by Ronald Syme

illustrated by William Stobbs

Today the name Verrazano graces the world's largest suspension bridge. Completed in 1964, it spans New York Harbor, first discovered by this Italian explorer during his memorable voyage of 1524. Here is the story of that voyage and the man who was responsible for it.

Born into a prosperous Florentine family who lived in France, Verrazano chose to become a seaman. By the age of twenty-three he was given his first command and began to transport cargoes across the Mediterranean Sea. Soon he turned his attention to the North Atlantic, seeking a westward route that would lead to the silks and spices of China. Sponsored by Florentine merchants in France and encouraged by the French king, Verrazano set forth. The first landfall turned out to be present-day Wilmington, North Carolina, and he proceeded to explore 2000 miles northward along the coast, keeping a valuable journal of all that he observed.

Vigorously illustrated, this biography dramatizes Verrazano's accomplishment and is a welcome addition to the scanty information available about this great event in North American history.

VERRAZANO

EXPLORER
OF THE ATLANTIC COAST

by Ronald Syme
illustrated by William Stobbs

William Morrow and Company
New York 1973

c

Printed in the United States of America.
1 2 3 4 5 77 76 75 74 73

Syme, Ronald, 1910–
    Verrazano, explorer of the Atlantic Coast.
    SUMMARY: A biography of the Italian who explored the Atlantic Coast from Cape Fear to Cape Breton discovering New York and Narragansett bays during his voyages.
    1. Verrazzano, Giovanni da, 1485?–1527—Juvenile literature. 2. America—Discovery and exploration—French—Juvenile literature. [1. Verrazzano, Giovanni da, 1485?–1527. 2. America—Discovery and exploration—French] I. Stobbs, William, illus. II. Title.
E133.V5S9   973.1′8′0924   [B]   [92]   72-7130
ISBN 0-688-20056-1
ISBN 0-688-30056-1 (lib. ed.)

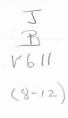

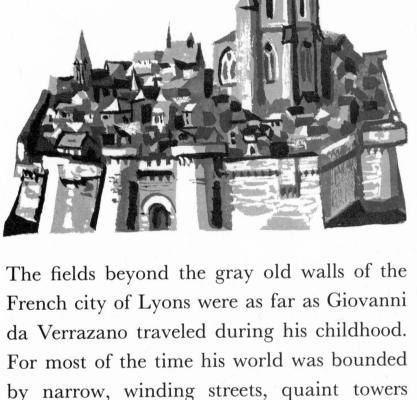

The fields beyond the gray old walls of the French city of Lyons were as far as Giovanni da Verrazano traveled during his childhood. For most of the time his world was bounded by narrow, winding streets, quaint towers perched on top of angular houses, and the dark little factories in which silk was woven on clattering handlooms from morning to night, six days a week.

And yet, Giovanni never thought of Lyons

as his real home. His family came from the brighter, warmer country of Italy, which lay on the other side of the high peaks of the Alps. The family home was located in Florence, five hundred miles away when measured in a straight line.

The household in Lyons consisted of Giovanni, his younger brother, Gerolamo, and their parents. Like many other ambitious citizens of Florence, Alessandro da Verrazano and his young wife, Fiammetta Capella, had chosen to settle in France. The Florentine merchants, bankers, industrialists, artists, and architects were respected and made welcome almost anywhere in Europe during the early 1500's. Being shrewd and highly educated men, the Florentines cared little in which country they lived as long as they could flourish in art or commerce. Giovanni's father had learned the silk-weaving industry as a young man in Florence. Now he owned three small factories in Lyons. The delicate and beautiful material they produced was in constant demand among the wealthy people.

Unlike most young Florentines, however, Giovanni and Gerolamo lacked a natural interest in business. Gerolamo, who was the more studious, was clever with pen and paper and enjoyed sketching maps. Giovanni had no similar recreation. He merely longed to travel and to visit some warmer country with brighter skies than those of central France. His restless nature was abruptly soothed in the year 1490 when he was already ten years old.

"We are all going on a visit to Florence," his father told the two boys. "It's time that you both see your native country and visit your grandparents."

"Are we going by land or sea?" asked Gerolamo, thinking perhaps of his beloved maps.

"By sea," replied his father. "We will travel

down the Rhône River to its mouth and thence by ship to Genoa. From Genoa to Florence we will travel by coach. The whole journey should not take us more than two or three weeks if everything goes according to schedule."

After the family's safe arrival in Florence on that unforgettable first journey in the spring-time of the year, Giovanni was soon wishing that he could remain there for the rest of his life. Never before had he seen so much beauty, a sky so blue, or such bright, cheerful, and industrious people. His grandparents' house, which stood some distance outside the city, was old even in those days. Its white stone walls formed three sides of a square around a central paved courtyard. Flowers and shrubs bloomed in the warm air. The roof was made of rustic brown tiles, and a tall grove of cypress trees almost hid the family homestead from view.

"You are not by any means the first visitor

to Florence who has fallen under the charm of our city," said Giovanni's grandfather, a wealthy and kindly old banker. "Lyons, which I visited years ago, seems to have grown carelessly over the centuries. It is not yet a city that has developed a soul of its own."

Grandfather Verrazano always spoke proudly of Florence, but then so did every other Florentine whom Giovanni met. The people seemed intensely proud of their lovely city. They had reason to be.

The domes and spires of Florence glittered in the smokeless air. The surrounding slopes of the Apennine Mountains reached up almost to the stout, surrounding walls. The green hillsides were covered with vineyards, olive trees, and white-walled, red-roofed villas. In the distance lay the silver thread of the Arno River, approaching the city through a beautiful valley. Along the city's wide streets walked Michelangelo, Botticelli, and Leonardo da

Vinci, whose names were to become immortal. The exquisite dome of the great cathedral had taken architects twenty-five years to design. In the gossamer mists of an autumn sunrise it resembled a vast gilded rosebud floating above the sweeping avenues, graceful colonnades, and palaces that formed the splendid background.

"There is no place as lovely as Florence in all the world," Alessandro da Verrazano said dreamily one day. Giovanni believed him. There *could* be no other city to match Florence.

Giovanni was silent and unhappy when the time came to say good-bye to his grandparents and to begin the long and tedious journey back to France. His downcast face soon attracted attention.

"We will come back here in a year or two," his father said comfortingly, "for I can never forget that Florence is my native city. I know you feel the same way, my son, and I hope that

you and Gerolamo are going to spend much
time here as part of your education."

On their arrival back in Lyons, Giovanni
gazed at the French city with critical and
unfriendly eyes, almost as if he never had seen
the place before.

Lyons stood on the right bank of the Saône
River at its junction with the mightier Rhône
River, which flowed down from the Swiss Alps
away to the north. The city had been growing

since the days when it was a Roman town. Many of its buildings were already hundreds of years old, and they had not always aged gracefully. Walls were inclined to be crooked, roofs sagged under the weight of their tiles, grass and weeds sprouted in odd corners. The muddy streets seemed narrow and even smellier than he remembered them.

No wonder, thought Giovanni, that the city had been saved from commercial stagnation only by the arrival of the Florentines and their creation of silk factories. The growing revenues from that trade were one of the many reasons why the king of France displayed warm friendship toward these foreigners who had chosen to settle in his country. But not even the thought of enjoying royal patronage in future years impressed Giovanni. All he wanted to do was to leave Lyons as soon as possible and hasten southward again to that lovely, glittering city beyond the Alps.

While Giovanni grew older and the silk looms of Lyons continued to clatter in the factories, maritime explorers began the wonderful age of discovery of unknown coastlines of the world. Christopher Columbus had reached the western shores of the Atlantic Ocean. Vasco da Gama had discovered the sea route to India. Amerigo Vespucci, a Florentine, had announced to startled geographers his belief that "the lands discovered by Signor Columbus are not the eastern coast of Cathay (China). Another continent, which we have never believed to exist, may lie between us and Cathay. On the western side of that ocean there may be another ocean."

When Giovanni Verrazano was seventeen years old, he finally decided on his future career. Although his grandparents were no longer alive, he continued to make frequent trips to Italy. From other relatives in Florence he had learned that the city had a fine school where,

among many other subjects, young men could receive a sound training in the art of navigation. After they had qualified, these young men became merchant sea captains. Giovanni decided to become a seaman.

These navigators could take their ships from one end of the Mediterranean to the other without mishap, a great achievement in those days, when even the best charts contained small but dangerous errors. Lighthouses were almost unknown, shoals and rocks were unmarked, treacherous currents were unlisted, and many of the harbors lacked all facilities. Being well educated and thoroughly trained, the sea captains kept their countrymen ashore well informed of the latest news in all the countries they visited.

From the time he was eighteen until he was twenty-one, Giovanni Verrazano lived in Florence and studied the classics, higher mathematics, and navigation. Later he was joined by Gerolamo, who, although not interested in a sea career, had decided to become a geographer.

Giovanni was at sea before his twenty-second birthday, as junior officer in a small Genoese galley. A year later he was given his first command. It was another humble, seagoing galley, propelled by a bank of oars, but it had a great lateen, or triangular, sail for use when the wind was favorable. In command of

this unstable and not very seaworthy craft, Giovanni learned all the finer points of seamanship.

By this time he was a darkly bearded young man of rather less than average height. He had strong, well-shaped features and widely set, imaginative eyes. Perhaps because he had not been brought up in the gay and lighthearted environment of Florence, he lacked the usual good humor and cheerfulness of his fellow-countrymen. But he had always been inclined toward silence and serious thought. During his years at sea he wrote few letters, formed few lasting friendships, and chose not to marry. Like Gerolamo, he had a tremendous interest in all the new maps that the geographers continued to produce as men's knowledge of the world increased.

"It was during my early years at sea," Verrazano wrote in later years, "that I acquired a great wish to undertake some new voyage of discovery that would bring fresh honors to my native city of Florence and perhaps some further increase of industry to the Florentine settlement in Lyons."

The cargoes that Verrazano sought most eagerly were bales of raw silk and bags of rare spices or incense, which reached the warehouses of Alexandria, Beirut, and Tyre. These goods came by caravan and less frequently by Arab dhow all the way from Cathay and the unknown islands that lay in tropical seas to the south, seen only by the famous traveler, Marco Polo. The silk was greatly in demand among the wealthier classes. The spices were necessary in every household in order to improve—or camouflage—the taste of badly preserved meat. The incense was used everywhere for religious purposes. Thus the whole of civilized Europe provided eager markets for the cargoes that Verrazano and his fellow-captains brought westward across the Medi-

terranean to the coasts of Italy, France, and Spain.

The years continued to pass. Verrazano was promoted to a larger trading vessel. He learned that navigators had explored almost the entire length of the east coast of South America. Portuguese seamen had discovered a sea route to the Spice Islands (Moluccas) in 1511, the year in which Verrazano was thirty-one years old. But unknown to him as yet, these hardy

Portuguese, with little care for the woes of other nations, were beginning to establish complete mastery of the Indian Ocean. Methodically they were cutting arteries of commerce up the Red Sea, across the desert, and through the Persian Gulf. Verrazano was one of those who soon began to feel the effects of the Portuguese activities. He wrote:

In the year 1518, I could purchase no spices at Alexandria or Beirut. The Portuguese have

19

so greatly increased the number of their ships proceeding to the Spice Islands, and have so much extended their influence in those same islands, that most of the spices were carried by their vessels direct to Portugal.

Verrazano's problems increased with each voyage he made.

"No pepper, no cinnamon, and no silk have come into our warehouses for months," his agents reported. "The Portuguese have robbed us of our trade. Cotton, olive oil, a few cases of dates, and some barrels of dried figs are the cargoes we can provide for you."

Alarm for the future soon began to spread among the merchants of Florence and especially of Lyons. Their supplies of raw materials were dwindling steadily. Some of their busy, clacking looms were slowing to a standstill. The only silk supplies available came from Portugal, and the hard-bargaining merchants of Lisbon were demanding extravagant prices.

Giovanni and Gerolamo discussed the future when they chanced to meet ashore. They were moody and discontented during the winter months when the Mediterranean was too rough and dangerous for trading voyages. Gerolamo felt that France had been left behind in the race among the nations of Europe to obtain overseas possessions. He also believed that the Mediterranean was ceasing to be the important sea that it had been for hundreds of years. The Atlantic Ocean would soon replace it. Giovanni's ideas were much the same; he longed more than ever to set forth on some voyage of exploration that might bring both glory and profit to Italy and France.

During one of their discussions, Gerolamo happened to glance at a chart of the Atlantic Ocean, which was lying on the table beside him. Prepared by a famous geographer named Apianus in 1520, the chart showed the bare

outline of the east coast of South America and many of the islands and mainland coasts of the Caribbean as well. But the east coast of North America was merely a wavering and uncertain outline. Obviously Apianus had used his imagination in charting the coast north of Florida.

"Magellan has set out to prove that a ship can sail westward across the world," said Gerolamo, "taking his little fleet around Cape

Horn. Is it not possible that an unknown channel, lying much farther to the north, also leads westward into the Pacific Ocean? Perhaps an undiscovered sea route may lie somewhere north of Florida."

"The Spanish have never explored that cold northern coast," said Giovanni. "No one has any idea of what may lie up there except perhaps a few French and English fishermen, and the master mariner, John Cabot, now gone."

In the spring of 1522, Giovanni resumed his trading voyages with the help of the returning, good northwest wind that blew steadily throughout the summer months. Gerolamo, the geographer, hastened north to Lyons and to Paris with his head full of new ideas. The east coast of North America was becoming very important to him.

In Paris, Gerolamo discussed that coast with the most learned geographers in the city. Because he was a Florentine and a man who was already making his mark in the world of charts and geographical learning, he was accorded an audience with King Francis the First in the royal palace. Seated in the king's private study, Gerolamo revealed what he knew about the oceans and sea routes of the world. The audience was interrupted for a brief time while a messenger was dispatched south across France to find Giovanni, who was commanded to make his way to Paris without delay.

The two brothers again visited the royal study. This time Giovanni was the one who spoke of his theory that the discovery of some entirely new passage to Cathay and the alluring Spice Islands was possible.

The king was fascinated. As Giovanni, burly, tanned, and bearded, continued to reveal his enormous knowledge of seafaring matters, the monarch's shrewd and watchful eyes remained steady on his face.

A senior Portuguese official wrote in the late summer of 1522:

A certain Florentine, João Verrazano, is with the king in France. He is proposing to the king a plan for a voyage of discovery to the eastern lands unknown to the Portuguese.

The information was accurate. Francis was greatly impressed by the information he had received from the Verrazano brothers. He hesitated to sponsor the voyage of discovery they proposed, for he knew well that any such scheme would arouse the fierce jealousy of Spain and Portugal. But there was nothing to prevent him from encouraging the Florentine merchants to promote such a voyage. Being a shrewd man, the king reflected that if other countries displayed too much fury at the idea, he could always plead that he had not been fully informed and that the Florentines must have exceeded the permission he had given.

Through Giovanni, the king let it be known to the merchants of Lyons that he was in favor of an attempt to discover a sea route across North America that might lead onward to the teeming warehouses and wealthy coast of China. The discovery of such a passage would enable France to send her ships to the Far East by a route much shorter than the Portuguese were using around the Cape of Good Hope and across the Indian Ocean.

This same idea had also occurred to King John the Third of Portugal. In a peevish letter to King Francis, he declared that Verrazano's proposed voyage would be nothing less than a poaching expedition on Portuguese territory. Was not the king aware that, by a decree issued by the Pope in 1493, the Atlantic Ocean was declared to belong to the Portuguese for a distance of about 1100 miles west of the Cape Verde Islands? (Westward of that imaginary line, all lands and oceans were declared to

belong to Spain.) Wherever this Verrazano proposed to go, added the Portuguese king, he would certainly be trespassing on the seas and probably the territories of Portugal or Spain. Would King Francis please ensure, therefore, that Verrazano was forbidden to make any such voyage?

The Florentines, being a proud-spirited people, never had thought very much of this Papal edict. French fishermen, far out in the

Atlantic, had always disregarded it. So had the English mariners during the few voyages they had made. King Francis decided to take the same attitude; he merely ignored King John's plaintive letter and gave permission for Verrazano's voyage to be made. While he would provide the ships, he expected the Florentines to finance the venture.

The names of the subscribers are still recorded in a written agreement dated 1523. The French officials, with their national dislike of any language other than their own, spelled the Florentine names in French style. They include Thomassin Gadaigne, Guillaume Naze, Robert Albisse, Antoine Gondy, and Julien Bonorcy. A number of wealthy Frenchmen also took shares in the venture. Among them was Jean Ango, a nobleman of Dieppe, who owned a private fleet that included merchant ships and fishing vessels. The plans of these earnest and generous financiers were encouraged by the great news they received: Magellan's ship, *Victoria,* had returned to Spain, though Magellan himself had been killed during the voyage and the rest of his ships destroyed. Now all men knew for a fact that it was possible to sail around the world.

The spring of the year 1523 produced wild gales and furious seas in the Atlantic Ocean. The four ships provided by the king fidgeted uneasily at their moorings in Dieppe. Day after day passed without any improvement in the weather. Verrazano, who distrusted the sea-keeping qualities of his two largest ships, refused to give the order to sail.

João da Silveira, the Portuguese ambassador, wrote on April 23, 1523:

> Master João Verrazano, who is going out to discover Cathay, has, at the time of writing this letter, not yet left. According to the information that I have, this delay is on account of weather

conditions. I have also heard that there are other doubts (or disagreements) between him and certain officers of the royal service.

The ambassador was well informed. King Francis had become involved in a dispute with Spain. The two countries were on the verge of declaring war. Some of the king's officials already had hinted to Verrazano that his ships might have to be reclaimed, "as it seems that his Illustrious Majesty may have need of such vessels to patrol the coast of Spain."

Verrazano, standing on the deck of the little *Dauphine,* the smallest of the four vessels but the one in which he had chosen to sail, was curt toward these unsympathetic officials.

"If the king, our lord, desires that I return to him these ships which he has granted me for this voyage, then let him inform me by royal command," he declared. "If I do not receive such command then I will sail, God

willing, when the waves no longer hurl solid masses of water against yonder sea wall."

In May the weather began to improve. Verrazano gave the order to make sail. The four ships edged out of the wide and ill-sheltered harbor of Dieppe and headed for the gray emptiness of the foam-streaked ocean.

Another tremendous gale came sweeping out of the west almost before the ships were off the southern coast of England. They were driven

apart by gale-force winds and forced to return to the safety of the port they had just left. For two days and nights, Verrazano and Antoine de Conflans, the silent, steady, veteran master of the *Dauphine,* fought to save their little vessel from the raging, towering waves. Accompanied by the *Normande,* a ship only slightly larger, the *Dauphine* finally made it back into port. The two larger vessels, which Verrazano had rightly eyed with distrust, went down with a loss of two hundred French seamen.

Another disappointment was awaiting Verrazano as he walked stiffly ashore, exhausted and encrusted with salt. French officials were waiting for him.

"We referred the matter of your vessels to the High Admiral," he was informed. "He has directed that all but the *Dauphine* must be handed back to the king's service without delay. We will therefore requisition the *Normande* at once and inform him that you have

had the misfortune to lose the two other vessels."

The little *Dauphine* was named for the young heir to the throne of France. She was a strongly built, three-masted ship of less than one hundred tons and had been built originally as a fishing vessel for use in the dangerous seas off the Newfoundland coast. At Verrazano's wish she had been rerigged and now carried lateen sails on at least two of her masts. From his experience in the Mediterranean, Verrazano knew what the shipbuilders of northern Europe were only beginning to suspect: that this type of sail was much more efficient and more easily handled. The *Dauphine* carried a crew of fifty men and enough rations for eight months.

The Florentine merchants were discouraged by the misfortunes of Verrazano's aborted expedition.

"Perhaps," they said, "it would be prudent to call off the voyage. Surely this one little vessel is too small to cross the Atlantic and, we hope, to sail onward to Cathay."

"The *Dauphine* was the fastest of the four ships with which I set out," Verrazano replied. "She survived a storm that sank two ships more than twice her size."

For the rest of the year 1523, Verrazano and Captain Conflans remained at Dieppe. The *Dauphine* was thoroughly repaired and overhauled. Into the remaining space in her hold were packed a few extra stores from the *Normande*. Early in January she was again ready to set out to sea. Beyond the stone breakwater of Dieppe harbor, the Atlantic Ocean lay cold, clear, and peaceful.

The Florentine merchants were still worried about the whole venture. They knew that the North Atlantic was infinitely more dangerous than the calmer seas of the tropics, and the small size of the *Dauphine* continued to alarm them.

"This ship will not betray us," said Verrazano in her defense. "With all the extra rations on board, she will not starve us, and Captain Conflans and I have already proved that she is unlikely to drown us. Let us be thankful for what we have."

The Florentines had still another source of worry. France and Spain were at war, they pointed out. There would be much hostility toward his voyage if the Spaniards knew—as perhaps they did—that he intended to sail to the coast of the American continent, which they regarded as their own. "We have let it be known, therefore," the merchants told Verrazano, "that you are sailing south to the coast of North Africa in order to attend to our business affairs. Please continue to give that impression when you leave Dieppe."

On January 2, 1524, the *Dauphine* put to sea. She steered southward until out of sight of land, then altered course slightly to the west. This south-by-west slant brought her ten days later to uninhabited Porto Santo Island near Madeira. Then she sailed again on January 17.

Verrazano set a course that he trusted would bring the *Dauphine* to the American coast in latitude thirty-two degrees north, or at Georgia and South Carolina. He wrote in his journal:

We will be hoping all the time to find some strait or real promontory where the land might

VERRAZANO'S VOYAGE OF 1524

50°

NEWFOUNDLAND

45°

CAPE BRETON ISLAND

NOVA SCOTIA

MAINE

VERMONT

N. H.

MASS.

NEW YORK

Hudson R.

CONN.

R.I.

40°

New York Bay

N. J.

MARYLAND

DEL.

Atlantic Ocean

Chesapeake Bay

Richmond

35°

VIRGINIA

N. CAROLINA

Cape Lookout

Wilmington

S. CAROLINA

30°

GEORGIA

25°

FLORIDA

Hudson R.

Upper Bay

The Narrows

Brooklyn

Staten Island

Lower Bay

New York Bay

end to the north, and we could reach those blessed shores of Cathay.

Thrusting along before what Verrazano described as "the gentle breeze of a light easterly wind," the *Dauphine* covered 2400 miles by February 11, just 25 days after leaving Porto Santo Island.

The science of navigation was rapidly improving throughout Europe, but in Verrazano's time—and for the next 250 years—the problem of measuring longitude, or distance east or west of Greenwich, continued to face all navigators and sometimes cost them their ships. Verrazano believed that he was undoubtedly more accurate in his results than most of those early navigators.

The longitudinal distance was known to us by navigating with various instruments, by the motion of the sun and by the distance the ship ran the various courses; thus we found the distance between one meridian (highest altitude of sun) and another geometrically.

With their charts, compass, and confidence Verrazano and Captain Conflans took the *Dauphine* across the Atlantic, covering a total distance of 3479 miles from Madeira. But as they were drawing in toward the coast, a tremendous storm came sweeping up from the south. The *Dauphine* was driven northward for 36 hours.

It was a storm as violent as ever sailing man encountered. We were delivered from it with the divine help and goodness of the ship, whose glorious name and happy destiny enabled her to endure the violent waves of the sea.

Verrazano must have known the age-old saying that a ship is no better than the men who sail her, but modesty prevented him from drawing attention to what must have been superb seamanship on the part of Captain Conflans and himself.

Wind and sea abated, but the favorable weather they had experienced during the earlier part of the voyage did not return. Verrazano's records show that during the first twenty-five days the ship sailed at an average speed of five and one-third nautical miles per hour. During the second twenty-five days, the *Dauphine* managed no better than two and two-thirds nautical miles an hour. Thus, the average speed for the entire voyage was four nautical miles an hour.

Rising up on a great roller, the men on the *Dauphine* caught their first glimpse of the American coast.

At first sight it appeared to be rather low lying. Having approached to within a mile, we realized that it was inhabited, for huge fires had been built on the seashore. We saw that the land stretched southward, and we coasted along

it in search of some port where we might anchor the ship and investigate the nature of the land, but in 50 leagues (190 miles) we found no harbor or place where we could stop with the ship.

Verrazano had reached land at thirty-four degrees north, or two degrees farther north than he had intended. The coast he sighted was that of present-day Wilmington on the coast of North Carolina. While searching for a sheltered harbor, he had gone as far south as he dared, for he had no wish to be sighted by the Spanish anywhere near Florida, to which part of North America they had made a very strong claim. Now he turned back north and began his task of exploration and search.

Verrazano's mood changed with his arrival in America. He began to reveal the sunny nature that had lain concealed for years beneath his reserve and silence. His reports became sensitive, light to read, and extremely observant. He took an interest in the Indians that was as rare as it was welcome, and he had the gift of being able to make friends with them. As a Florentine who loved beauty, he immediately could appreciate the green lushness of a forest or the fragile delicacy of some small flower. His account remains of tremendous historical value even today, for it was the earliest document to describe the country and the Indian tribes along the Atlantic coast north of Florida.

Not until the *Dauphine* hove-to off the long line of dunes stretching from Cape Lookout to Richmond in Virginia, however, did Verrazano make his first landing.

We had seen many people coming to the seashore, but they fled when they saw us approaching. Several times they stopped and turned round to look at us in great wonderment. We reassured them with various signs, and some of them came up, showing great delight at seeing us and marveling at our clothes, appearance, and our whiteness. They showed us by

various signs where we could most easily secure
the boat and offered us some of their food.

Verrazano was the first man to wade ashore
from the *Dauphine*'s boat and walk up the beach
to greet those Indians. Within a few minutes
his friendly smile and empty hands had con-
vinced them that here was no new and mortal
enemy. They crowded around him to peer at
his bearded face, his weatherbeaten black hat,

his heavy broadcloth clothing, and the silver-chased handle of the light sword he carried.

They go completely naked except that around their loins they wear skins of small animals like martens, with a narrow belt of grass around the body to which they tie various tails of other animals which hang down to the knees. . . . They are dark in color, with thick black hair, not very long, tied behind the head like a small tail. . . . They are well proportioned, of medium height, a little taller than we are. They have broad chests, strong arms, and the legs and other parts of the body are well formed. . . . They have big black eyes and an attentive and open look. . . . Nearby we could see a stretch of country much higher than the sandy shore, with many beautiful fields and plains full of great forests, and the trees have so many colors, are so beautiful and delightful that they defy description.

Verrazano and his companions were so interested in this first meeting that the business of refilling the water casks seems to have been neglected. After that long voyage across the Atlantic, the water remaining on board the ship must have had a musty, woody flavor, which would have made it undrinkable by anyone except those tough French seamen. But the result of this omission was that a few days later the ship paused off the coast of Virginia several hundred miles to the north. There Verrazano sent a boat ashore in search of a stream.

The sea was too rough to make a landing. While the sailors rested on their oars and wondered what to do, a number of Indians came running to the beach to stare in wonder.

We sent one of our young sailors swimming ashore to take the people some little bells, mirrors, and other trifles. When he came close he threw them the goods and tried to turn back. But he was so tossed about by the waves that he was carried up on the beach half dead. Seeing this, the native people immediately ran up. They took him by the arms and dragged him some distance away. Whereupon the youth, realizing he was being carried away, was seized with terror and began to utter loud cries. . . . They answered him in their language to show him he should not be afraid. . . . They took off his shirt and shoes, leaving him naked, then made a huge fire next to him, placing him near the heat.

The sailors on the *Dauphine,* who were unhappily watching the scene on the beach, began to shout that the savages were preparing to roast their comrade. The kindness with which the Indians had dragged the half-drowned man from the surf meant nothing to them. Soon, however, they realized that their suspicions had been unjust.

After remaining with them for a while, the young man regained his strength and showed them by signs that he wanted to return to the ship. With the greatest kindness they accompanied him to the sea, holding him close and embracing him. Then, to reassure him, they withdrew to a high hill and stood watching until he was in the boat.

Past a coast that was "very green and forested but without harbors," the *Dauphine* sailed onward while the crew scanned the coast in search of a successful landing. On the coast of Virginia they sighted a small cove, where the boat was able to reach the shore without diffi-

culty. Verrazano, as usual, accompanied this boat.

We found a man who came to the shore to see who we were. He stood suspiciously and ready for flight. He watched us but would not come near. He was handsome, naked, with olive-colored skin, his hair fastened back in a knot. There were about twenty of us ashore, and we coaxed him. He approached to within about twelve feet of us and showed us a burning stick as if to offer us fire. We lit some powder with a flint, and he trembled all over with fear as we fired a shot. He remained as if thunderstruck and prayed, worshiping like a monk. Pointing with his finger to the sky and indicating the sea and the ship, he appeared to bless us.

Pipes and tobacco were still unknown in Europe. The Indian was merely offering Verrazano a chance to enjoy a smoke.

To this green and lovely part of the Virginia coast, Verrazano gave the name of Arcadia.

The land is like the previous one in fertility and beauty, but the woods are sparse. The land is covered with different types of trees, but they are not so fragrant, since it is more northern and cold. We saw there many vines growing wild. They would doubtless produce excellent wines if they were properly cultivated, for several times we found the dry fruit sweet and pleasant, not unlike our own.

The water casks were filled again. While at

sea, the water ration was less than a gallon per man per day for all purposes, including cooking. Sailing along this coast, the crew of the *Dauphine* reveled in the copious supply of fresh water now available to them.

Due to the fading evening light, or perhaps a rain squall, Verrazano failed to notice the entrance to Chesapeake Bay. The *Dauphine* sailed onward, passing the Atlantic shores of Maryland, Delaware, and New Jersey. After sighting the Navesink Highlands, which Verrazano named San Polo, to the south of Sandy Hook, he suddenly sighted the entrance to New York Bay.

> We found a very agreeable place between two small but prominent hills. Between them a wide river, deep at its mouth, flowed out into the sea. . . . We took the small boat up this river to land, which we found densely populated. The people were dressed in birds' feathers of various colors, and they came toward us joyfully, uttering loud cries of wonderment and

showing us the safest place to beach the boat. We went up this river for about a mile and a half, where we saw that it formed a beautiful lake, about nine miles in circumference.

It was on April 17, 1524, that Verrazano and his jersey-clad French seamen stepped ashore from their sturdy little sailing boat at Tompkinsville at the northern end of Staten Island. They had left the *Dauphine* riding safely at anchor in the channel between the southern end of Staten Island and the Jersey coast. The two "small but prominent hills" that Verrazano sighted were Grymes Hill and Emerson Hill. The West Shore Expressway runs past them today.

Delighted with the friendly welcome they were receiving, Verrazano reentered the boat and sailed on through the fast-running waters of the Narrows into the Upper Bay. Directly ahead of them the entrance to the Hudson River became visible in the clear, sparkling

air. But at that moment fate decreed that Verrazano was not to be the first European to sight the great river.

Suddenly, as often happens in sailing, a violent, unfavorable wind blew in from the sea and we were forced to return to the ship, leaving the land with much regret on account of its favorable conditions and beauty. We think it not without some properties of value, since all the hills showed signs of minerals.

Verrazano was a careful and observant explorer, but first and foremost he was the commander of the *Dauphine*. Doing what any good seaman would in similar circumstances, he made sure that the *Dauphine*'s anchor cable was holding in the face of that sudden squall and that the ship was in no danger. But once he was back in his cabin, he continued to write his impressions of this tremendous bay.

These people are the most beautiful and have the most civil customs that we have found on this voyage. They are taller than we are. They are of a bronze color, some tending more toward whiteness, others to a tawny color. The face is clear-cut, the hair is long and black, and they take great care to decorate it. Their eyes are black and alert, and their manner is sweet and gentle. . . . Their women are just as shapely and beautiful, very gracious, of attractive manner and pleasant appearance. They go nude except for a stag skin embroidered like the men's, and some wear rich lynx skins on their arms. . . . We saw that they had many sheets of worked copper, which they prize more than gold. They do not value gold because of its color; they think it the most worthless of all and rate blue and red above all other colors.

Verrazano never sailed his boat again into the Upper Bay. The Hudson River remained unknown to Europe for another eighty-five years. Not until September 6, 1609, did Henry Hudson in his *Half Moon* steer through the

Narrows and drop anchor in New York Bay, not far from the future site of the Statue of Liberty.

Verrazano gave the name Angoulême to New York Bay and the countryside around it. This designation was a polite compliment to King Francis, one of whose titles in France was Count of Angoulême. The Upper Bay he called the Bay of Saint Marguerite, naming it after the king's sister, "who surpasses all other matrons in modesty and intellect."

The full report written by Verrazano creates a splendid word picture of these New York Indians. He described their canoes, their cleverly built round huts, and the "worked mats of straw which protect them from wind and rain." He noted the care and respect they showed toward their women, admired the fine workmanship of their arrows tipped with hard marble, and wrote approvingly of the "cherries, plums, and filberts, and many kinds of

fruit different from ours." At the end of his report, Verrazano, as modest as ever, concluded with the words: "This is all that we could learn of them."

On May 6 the *Dauphine* left New York, much to the regret of everyone on board.

We weighed anchor and sailed eastward since the land veered in that direction, and we covered 450 miles, always keeping in sight of the land.

The rest of that voyage along the American coast was much less interesting. The temperature dropped daily, and the land grew less attractive. The local Indian tribes resembled the stark area in which they lived.

> They were full of crudity and vices and were so barbarous that we could never make any communication with them, however many signs we made to them.

The coast of Maine was the first locality in which the crew needed to carry weapons whenever they went ashore in search of water. These unfriendly Indians sometimes "shot at us with their bows and uttered loud cries before fleeing into the woods."

Verrazano's voyage of exploration finally came to an end. Since first sighting land he had explored over 2000 miles of completely unknown coast. He knew his work was done when he reached "the land which the Britons

once found, which lies in 50 degrees." This entry was a reference to John Cabot's visit to Newfoundland in the year 1497. Cabot had explored 1000 miles of coast without finding any channel that led to the west.

The *Dauphine* turned her stern toward North America and began the long voyage across the Atlantic back to France. Verrazano had failed to discover a passage to Cathay, but he closed the last gap in men's knowledge of the coast from Patagonia to Labrador. He brought back the first descriptions of the Indians of North America. This information, perhaps under-rated at the time, was what caused a modern geographer to declare: "Verrazano's account is the most accurate and the most valuable of all the early coastal voyages that have come down to us."

With favorable winds and weather, the *Dauphine* reached Dieppe on July 8, 1524. Verrazano had completed his report, which

was written in his native Italian language. It was duly translated into French and dispatched to the king. Other copies of the original Italian version were sent to Florence for reading by Verrazano's family and friends.

Gerolamo was one of the first visitors to the *Dauphine*. From what Giovanni was able to tell him, and by studying the charts his brother had prepared, Gerolamo realized that the earlier much-respected maps produced by learned geographers were wrong in many instances. These learned men, prompted by wishful thinking instead of accurate knowledge, had shown an open and navigable channel leading westward across North America from the Atlantic Ocean. Gerolamo, like Giovanni, now realized that if any such passage existed, it could lie only in some undiscovered locality along the western shore of the Caribbean Sea.

One of the new maps soon to be prepared by Gerolamo found its way into the possession of King Henry the Eighth of England. Sixty years later one of the first and most famous of English geographers, Richard Hakluyt, wrote of "an olde excellent mappe which Master John Verrazano gave to King Henrie the Eighth." This map quite possibly helped to awaken in England the spirit of maritime exploration that was to inspire the country for the next 300 years.

The Florentine merchants were disappointed with the results that Verrazano had obtained. Coastlines and Indians were all very well, but what they needed desperately was a handy sea route to the Far East. For the time being they abandoned the idea of financing another voyage.

King Francis, with a display of common sense that was lamentably unusual among monarchs, recognized that Verrazano was a competent and daring navigator who deserved to be encouraged as an explorer. Delighted with this display of royal favor, Verrazano, in 1526, was again at work on plans for a fresh voyage. Wealthy and influential Frenchmen were eager to provide financial assistance. Admiral Philippe de Chabot, one of the most respected men in France, became Verrazano's patron and advisor.

"The Mediterranean silk trade is finished," Verrazano told him bluntly. "No more silk and incense will come by that route. In any case, we had to pay for these goods with gold and silver, which we could ill afford."

The exports of France and Italy were unacceptable to the merchants of the Levant. Tiles and machinery, barrels of tar, and cannon were too heavy to be transported by camel caravan across the Isthmus of Suez and then to the Far East. But the Portuguese could load their ships in Lisbon with those same items, then sail across half the world and deliver them to the very ports where the silk and incense were available.

"We have lost the race with the Portuguese so far to pay for our imports with our own exports," Verrazano declared. "If we use the sea route around Africa, the Portuguese will be swift to resent the presence of our ships. A shorter and quicker sea route to the Indies would restore the wavering fortunes of France."

Admiral Chabot decided that the shortest passage to the Spice Islands was by way of the strait that Magellan had used to pass into the Pacific Ocean. "We will use it for at least the first expedition that France sends out. Spain has no settlement so far south; the Spanish cannot declare that we are trespassing on their possessions in the New World."

"Giovanni Verrazano, nobleman, captain of ships," as he was described in official documents, sailed in June, 1526. He was now forty-six years old, an advanced age in those days. His hair and beard were turning gray, but mentally and physically he had changed little since the days when he was the captain of a Mediterranean trading vessel. His burning interest in exploration seemed to be keeping him young.

The record of that second voyage is limited and incomplete. The kings of those days had the habit of moving from one royal castle to

another, seldom spending more than a few months in any one residence. The unlucky officials in charge of the royal archives had to pack up and convey wagonloads of material to the king's latest residence. Many records and documents were lost during these moves, and some were never noticed at the time or recovered later. Nearly all the papers in connection with Verrazano's second voyage are missing from the French collection of national

historical files. Only the bare facts of the story have been unearthed by modern historians.

Verrazano led his three ships, all of which were larger than the *Dauphine,* from the mouth of the Amazon River southward to the vicinity of Magellan Strait. Gerolamo accompanied him this time, being curious to see for himself the coastlines and countries he had scanned so often on charts.

A series of gales kept Verrazano from passing through the Strait, a piece of navigation that was dangerous even in the best of weather. He finally ordered the ships to put about and to steer across the Atlantic to the Cape of Good Hope. He had made up his mind that if the weather prevented him from reaching the Spice Islands by the westerly route, then he would attempt to arrive at his destination by the easterly route across the Indian Ocean.

In that winter of 1526, the weather off the Cape was at its worst. Instead of the prevailing westerly winds, a succession of easterly gales piled up fifty-foot waves that battered the struggling vessels. Nevertheless, after several weeks, one of Verrazano's ships managed to pass eastward into the Indian Ocean. His own vessel and the one with Gerolamo on board were unable to follow.

Verrazano decided to give up this apparently endless struggle. He knew that the two ships could not continue to endure such

buffeting; indeed, they were already leaking and their timbers were straining to the utmost. "We will sail westward again," he said. "When we reach the coast of South America, we will load up with brazilwood and return to France. Our cargo will at least cover the cost of the voyage."

Brazilwood, from which was produced a valuable scarlet dye, grew along the northern coast of Brazil and also in some of the Spanish islands of the West Indies. Verrazano's weary seamen, sweating in the damp heat of the tropical forest, cut and loaded the timber and sailed back to France. They arrived on September 15, 1527, after a voyage that had lasted 15 months and during which he had covered a total distance of 20,000 miles.

Diego de Gouveia, a Portuguese official in France, wrote:

Master Giovanni Verrazano, who was captain of three ships destined for the Indies, has re-

turned with his brother. The reason for it is that the sailors, when they saw themselves caught in the tempest near the Cape, insisted on having their own way with his ship and that of his brother. As to the third ship, they say it has passed beyond (the Cape) without there being any more news of it. These (Giovanni and Gerolamo) went along the coast of Brazil and there loaded the brother's ship and that of Master Giovanni Verrazano with brazilwood.

Gouveia was a reliable official who usually got his facts straight. According to him, Giovanni had been faced with the threat of mutiny aboard his ship. This report may well have been true, for seamen in those days were rough and undisciplined. Much of the rest of his story was confirmed later by Antonio de Silveira de Meneses, the viceroy of the Portuguese settlement of Moçambique on the east coast of Africa.

This official, in a report that was only discovered in 1958, stated that the remaining ship

managed to reach the island of Sumatra in the
East Indies. The Frenchmen were then at-
tacked by the natives, who came darting
alongside the ship in their fast canoes. A number of the seamen, including the invaluable
pilot, were killed. The survivors decided to
return to Africa. Shorthanded and unsure of
their navigation, they were wrecked on a
sandbank near Madagascar. They kept themselves alive on turtles, coconuts, and birds' eggs

while they ingeniously built a small boat. Then they sailed this little craft to Moçambique.

The Portuguese, a hard but humane people, provided food and shelter for the twelve Frenchmen who came ashore. One hundred and forty other seamen had lost their lives during the whole of this disastrous voyage.

Verrazano's reputation still remained high throughout France. The Florentine bankers and merchants now came forward with an unexpected offer to finance a third voyage.

"What we have in mind is dangerous," Verrazano was warned bluntly. "It is nothing less than a voyage into the Spanish territories of the West Indies. So many geographers in recent years have indicated a western passage that we cannot bring ourselves to accept that no such passage exists."

"If it does, then you are right. It must be somewhere along the western shore of the

Caribbean Sea itself," Verrazano replied. "I have searched the eastern coast of the whole continent of America and found nothing. If you wish me to go there, I will in spite of the Spanish."

The Portuguese ambassador in France soon was reporting to the king of Portugal:

> Verrazano leaves here with five ships which the Admiral Chabot has ordered to sail to a great river on the coast of Brazil, which, they say, was discovered by a Spaniard. . . . They said Verrazano will begin his voyage and depart in February or March (1528). . . . I think they are going to establish a base there, and thereafter they will push still farther with their exploration.

That the Portuguese had got hold of inaccurate information was not surprising. The French authorities and the Florentines were keeping very quiet about Verrazano's real destination in the Caribbean Sea.

Verrazano, though not very hopeful of finding a channel, was interested by a strange fact. Early voyagers in that sea had noticed a slight but perceptible current that ran always to the west. This current, they believed, might indicate an open passage leading to the Pacific. (It was actually the north equatorial current that flows into the southern Caribbean, curls northward along the coast of Mexico, and then runs eastward again past the southern tip of Florida to merge with the Gulf Stream.)

Peter d'Anghiera, an official at the Spanish court and one of the great geographers of the age, supported Verrazano's theory. "In a hidden corner of that great land to the west of Cuba," he declared, "openings must exist which receive these swift waters and discharge them to the westward."

Giovanni Verrazano set out on his last voyage in April, 1528, when he was forty-eight years old. With his five ships, all merchant

vessels chartered for the voyage, he set course toward Florida. After sighting that dangerous Spanish-owned peninsula, he passed on to the Bahama Islands, where the boats went ashore to gather fresh vegetables, green coconuts, and turtles. Back in France, King Francis, with the support of the entire French nation, already had challenged Pope Alexander the Sixth's Bull of Demarcation and the Treaty of Tordesillas, by which rights to all lands in the new worlds of Asia and America had been given to Portugal and Spain.

Verrazano went on southward past Puerto Rico to Trinidad. Off the mountainous coast of that island they turned west and began to cruise past the high green coast of Venezuela. Some of the men grumbled that Verrazano seemed to be in a great hurry and was granting no time for the vessel to swing at anchor in some sheltered haven for a night or two. His reply to them was direct.

"A night spent in harbor is half a day and a whole tide wasted, and it may mean an advance of forty miles thrown away. The more days we spend in this sea, the more likely the Spanish are to learn of our presence here. Why risk a sharp quarrel with the men of that country? Let us remember that the wages of sin—and laziness is a sin—can be death at sea."

And so the ships sailed on steadily until they came to the Gulf of Darien on the northwest

coast of South America. When they saw a small, forested island ahead, Verrazano brought the squadron in close to the shore and gave the order to anchor. He then swung himself into a boat and set off for the shore, intending perhaps to discover whether the island could provide fresh vegetables and water for the ship.

A small crowd of natives was waiting near the beach. Verrazano was ignorant of the fact that these embittered people were much given to the use of poison. More than twenty years earlier, Vasco Balboa had tasted the full bitterness of their hatred. Verrazano, who always had liked and befriended the Indian tribes of North America, probably assumed that they were much the same kind of people.

With his seamen coming along behind him, Verrazano walked up the white, pebbly beach with his hands outstretched in greeting. He was within a few yards of them when the natives stooped to seize the weapons they had concealed in the undergrowth at their feet. When they stood erect again, they were grasping bows and poisoned arrows and short, barbed spears.

Verrazano and his six seamen fell dead on the beach.

From the decks of their anchored ships, Gerolamo and his companions saw their leader fall. Shouting in great anger, the seamen

demanded permission to go ashore to avenge the murder.

After a hasty discussion, Gerolamo and the captains decided against the idea. A landing party, faced with elusive enemies in the dense jungle of that interior, would suffer heavy casualties and probably accomplish little. A few of the ships' guns were trained on the shore and fired, but the natives merely disappeared into the forest. There was nothing else that the Frenchmen could do.

The ships raised their anchors and hoisted sail. Shocked by the tragedy and bereft of Verrazano's trusted leadership, they sailed out of the Caribbean Sea. They paused on the coast of Brazil to collect cargoes of the valuable dyewood, and then sailed home to France. They reached Dieppe at the end of November, 1528.

Verrazano's death, though greatly mourned

throughout France and Italy at the time, gradually was forgotten. For three hundred years after his death, Verrazano's great achievements were mentioned only as confused legends and fragments of half-forgotten history. During the 1800's it became fashionable among historical writers to question and criticize the accomplishments of famous men who had lived in earlier ages. In 1864, a leading writer unkindly suggested that Verrazano probably had never made any worthwhile voyages at all. This unjustified statement was repeated by other writers during the next ten years. One of them went so far as to state that Verrazano had been hanged as a pirate by the Spanish in the year 1527.

The carelessness that existed among clerks and scribes during the centuries after Verrazano's death was partly to blame for these errors. Florin, a French pirate, was justly hanged by the Spanish in 1527. His name, written by these copyists, was sometimes spelled Florentin in official records. The French word *florentin* means a native of Florence. The writers of the 1800's decided that a Florentine had been hanged by the French authorities and that he must have been Verrazano. To support their opinions, they quoted a Spanish historian named Gonzales de Barcia, who had made a similar mistake by writing "Juan Verrazano, a native of Florence, a French corsair." This earnest Spaniard was probably one of the first to have been led astray by the careless spelling of the clerks.

In 1897, a respected Italian biographer suggested how this misunderstanding had arisen by producing a number of ancient documents, which he had discovered in the National Library of Lisbon. Several of these official records contained legal statements regarding the activities and sea career of Juan Florin, the corsair.

In 1900, the truth about Verrazano was made clear to the world. A great Italian scholar, Alessandro Bacchiani, discovered in a private Roman library a copy of Verrazano's original report of his first voyage. It was one of the copies, written in his native Italian, that the explorer had sent to his friends in Florence. In fact, it bore a number of small corrections and amendments written in Verrazano's own handwriting.

With the discovery of this splendid old document, now reposing in the Pierpont Morgan Library in New York, all doubts and uncertainties concerning Verrazano finally were banished. The Florentine was promptly acknowledged as the explorer who, in sailing through the Narrows, discovered New York Harbor.

In 1964, when the bridge connecting Staten Island with Brooklyn, between the Lower and Upper Bay was opened, it bore the name of

Verrazano. The Florentine, who loved the beauty created by man, undoubtedly would have admired this bridge, a magnificent creation of imagination and architecture.

Thus, more than four hundred years later, Verrazano's place in history is officially recognized. Today, his voyage of 1524 is considered to be one of the great events in the history of North American discovery.

BIBLIOGRAPHY

Bacchiani, Alessandro, *Giovanni da Verrazzano and His Discoveries in North America.* Rome: Bollettino della Società Geografica Italiana, 1909.

Burpee, Lawrence J., *The Discovery of Canada.* Toronto: The Macmillan Company of Canada Ltd., 1946.

Habert, Jacques, *La Vie et les Voyages de Jean de Verrazzano.* Ottawa: Le Cercle du Livre de France, 1964.

Lipinsky, Lino, *Giovanni da Verrazzano, the Discoverer of New York Bay* (based on a copy of the explorer's original report of his discoveries). New York, 1958.

Magnaghi, Alberto, *Amerigo Vespucci: Studio Critico.* Rome: Instituto Cristoforo Colombo, 1926.

Sykes, Percy (Sir), *A History of Exploration* (third edition). London: Routledge & Kegan Paul Ltd., 1949.

Triborough Bridge and Tunnel Authority, *Spanning the Narrows* (booklet). New York, 1964.

Wroth, Lawrence C., *The Voyages of Giovanni da Verrazzano, 1524–1528.* New Haven: Yale University Press, 1970.